This book began to come together about two years ago, and while a couple of patterns are ones that I designed decades ago,
these are some of my favorites.

My bucket list includes my wish to get all of my patterns into books before I "kick the bucket".

That is a fine goal, but a sure and certain
challenge since I just keep on designing new tatting patterns, and the old ones are all sitting there staring at me waiting their turn
to be added to a collection.

We're waiting... say the pigs, and snail, stars, and cicada, and, and, and...

The newer patterns have been a fun challenge to add to this collection.

Copyright © 2014 Rozella Florence Linden
All rights reserved

You may make as many items from patterns in this book as you wish.
You may sell your tatted items or give them away.

ISBN-13: 978-1591968713
ISBN-10: 1501068717

Shabby Chic Tatting

By

Rozella Florence Linden

Dedication

For Mary Adalade Larkcom Wheeler
and her daughters
Rozella, Florence, and Ada

I only met my great grandmother once when I was very little, but I grew up spending lots of time with my Grandmother, Zella, and my two great aunts.

Oh how we all enjoyed dinners at Grandma's house!

There were always home made treats including grandma's molasses cookies, stewed tomatoes, canned peaches, green beans, and pickles and relish of all kinds.

Be sure and save room for dessert!
We have apple pie, elderberry pie, mincemeat pie, cherry pie, peach pie, and of course coconut cake.

Table of Contents

Terms & Notation	2
Sunflower	4
Sunflower Edging	7
Vintage Rose & Leaf	8
Daisy	12
Six Petal Flower	13
Circle Flower & Table Mat	18
Tatted Table Cloth	20
Designing A Round Tablecloth	22
Tatted Wine Glass Marker	23
Three Flowers Heart	24
Tiny Beaded Heart	27
Clovers Heart	28
Heart Sachet	30
Pearl Butterfly	32
Heart Photo Frame	36
Square Photo Frame	41
Tatted Bedspread	42
Antique Edging and Insertion	46
Shell Edging	48
Shell Scarf or Table Runner	49
Pantry Shelf Vintage Lace	50
Ribbon & Flowers Lace	52
Ribbon & Flowers Lace Corner	56
Eight Split Ring Flower	57
Small Five Point Flower	58

Terms & Notation

DS	Tatting stitch or double stitch
BDS	Balanced double stitch DS with an extra turn around the core thread for each half of the stitch.
RDS	Reversed Double Stitch Wrapped stitches, like the second half of a split ring.
-	Picot
—	Long Picot used for making a double picot when joined to after tatting a few more stitches.
+	Join to a previously tatted picot
+-	Join with a picot. Do the first half of the join then make a picot by tatting a full DS.
Ring (2 – 2)	Tat a ring of. 2ds, a picot, 2ds, and then close the ring
B	Bead
B+	Add a Bead when making a join.
Split Ring	Ring that starts at one place and ends at another place.
Turn	Reverse work or flip it over
CTM	Continuous Thread Method – do not cut the thread between the ball and shuttle or betweeen two shuttles.
Chain ##	Tat a chain of ## ds ## indicates the number of ds to tat
THC	Tie the thread ends. Hide the ends. Cut them off.
Twisted Cord Picot	This is a picot with the thread twisted the same direction as the twist of the thread so that it twists into a single cord.

A great big thank you to my tatting friends who have helped test and review the instructions.

Thank you Joanne and Lottie for your help and patience with my slow progress on this project.

Hugs to you.

Tatting friends are the best friends!

I hope you all enjoy this collection of tatting patterns!

Ruth Perry
AKA Rozella Linden

Tatted Sunflower

Skill Level: Intermediate

Here is a pretty little sunflower to brighten up your day!

Shuttle one is brown. Wind the shuttle then cut the thread from the ball. Shuttle two is green. Wind the shuttle and then cut from the ball. The yellow thread is used from the ball.

Advanced Skills used include double picots and Balanced Double Stitch. Use a picot gauge to make the double picots so that they are all the same size. Using size 20 thread the picots should be ½" horizontal or ¼" vertical measure.

Begin tatting with S1 brown thread.
Ring 1 – 1 – 1 – 1 – 1 – 1

Make a false picot by using the thread tail and the shuttle thread. Leave the space of a picot and tat the 2nd half of the DS unflipped, then tat the second half DS flipped. This knot will not slide.

Leave a thread space about the same size as a picot.
Ring 1 MP 1 – 1 MP 1 + (join to first MP) 1 MP + 1

This photo shows the work thus far. The smaller, normal, picot is used for spacing. So, as you can see here, the double picots are just longer picots, that are joined to, three stitches later in this pattern.

Now we are ready to make the next Measured Picot. Continue in this pattern repeating the MP and joins until you have nine of the MP used for the double picots.

The next picot is a smaller normal picot. Join to the ninth MP to complete this ring. Close the ring, and then fold the first ring over the center of the second ring and pull the thread tail through the middle of ring and tie it to the shuttle thread to anchor it in place.

Using shuttle 1 (brown) and the ball thread (yellow)
tat the outside round of flower petals.

Chain 1 – 1 – 1 + (Join to the longer side of the first double picot) 1 – 1 – 1 + (join to the next double picot)

Repeat around until you have 18 yellow picots joined to the nine double picots of the center. Bring the shuttle thread around the thread tails and join to itself to complete the outside round of the flower.

Stem

Gather all of the thread ends together and add in the Shuttle two (Green) thread. Using S2 tat over all of the thread ends using unflipped balanced double stitches. After doing about 2 or 3 of the unflipped BDS separate the shortest of the thread tail threads, and continue over the remaining thread tails. After another 2 or 3, separate another thread tail, then do 2 or 3 more and separate the third thread tail.

There are NO thread ends to work in when you are finished. Continue as before tatting unflipped BDS with S2 (Green) over the remaining three threads; one brown, one green, and one yellow.

Leaves

When you have eight or ten of the unflipped BDS tatted for the stem turn the tatting over and tat a ring with just the S2 (Green) thread.

Ring 9 BDS, first ½ DS – 2nd half DS, 9 BDS, close the ring and turn. (This has a picot in the middle of the normal DS)

To finish the bookmark, tat a few more stem stitches and then tie the S2 thread in an overhand knot with the thread ends. Tighten the tension of the thread ends so that the green thread is the only thread color that shows. This will bring the green shuttle thread to the opposite side of the stem. Tat a few more stem BDS, then another leaf, then a few more stem BDS.

Tie a double overhand knot in all the thread ends including the green, and cut all of the thread ends to about 15" long. Finish the tail of the bookmark by making twisted cord.

Tatted Sunflower Edging

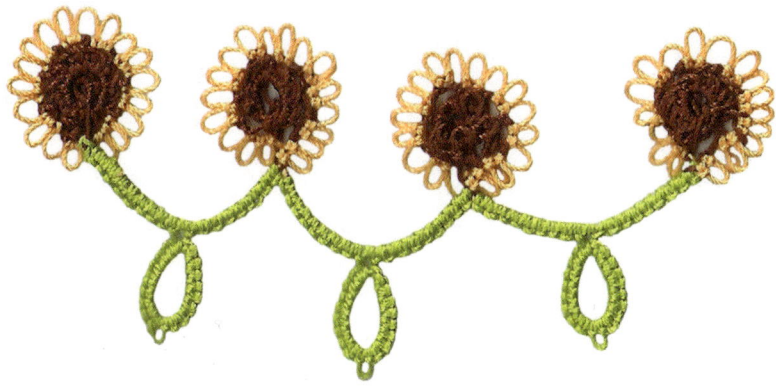

Complete the sunflower as in the bookmark, and the first nine unflipped BDS for the stem, hiding the thread ends as before. Turn the work and tat a leaf, and then turn and do nine more unflipped BDS.

Turn and begin another sunflower by leaving a small space, about ¼ " before tatting the first ring.

When the two brown rings for the center are completed, join to the thread space between the two brown rings to anchor the smaller ring in place.

   Repeat sunflowers and leaves for the length of edging desired.

Vintage Rose & Leaf

Rose Instructions

This looks simple, but it was one of the most challenging to tat! There is just one ring, and then the chains must have the correct proportions and shape for the flower to lie flat.

You may change the stitch counts as you tat to achieve the desired shape. Pull the thread just tight enough to make the correct shape of each chain section between the joins.

Wind about half a yard of thread onto a shuttle, CTM with the ball.

Ring A (1 - 4 – 3 – 2) turn

Chain 1 + 3 - 2 – 4 + 3 – 4 + 2 +-

This join is to the same picot as the previous join. It is shown by a blue X on the diagram.

To do the +- "join with a picot", make the first half of a lock join by pulling a loop of the thread up through the picot and then put the shuttle through the loop. Tighten it by pulling the thread so that the loop closes. Next, make a picot by tatting a full DS.

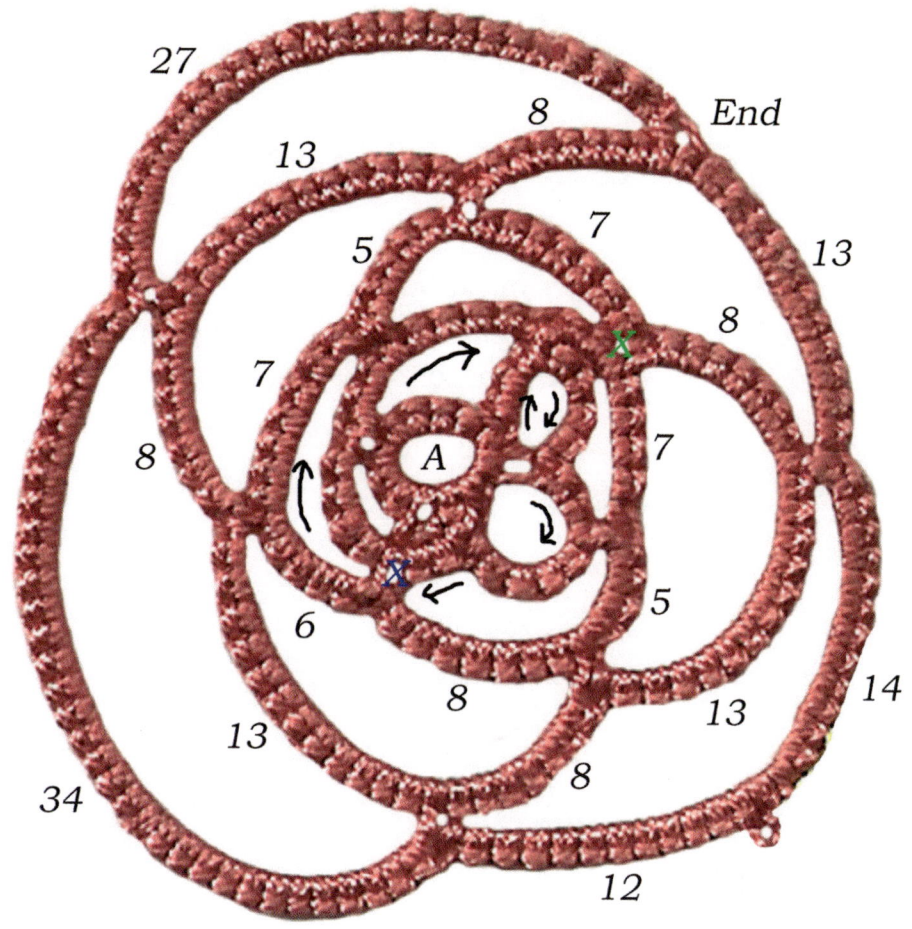

Continue tatting the chain…

4 + 3 – 6 + 3 +- [This join with a picot is shown with a green X]

7 + 5 – 8 + 6 – 8 + [This join is to the picot marked with the blue X]

6 – 7 + 5 – 7 + [This join is to the picot marked with the green X]

8 – 13 + 8 – 13 + 8 – 13 + 8 – 13 + 14 – 12 + 34 + 27

Tie the ends together in the next picot, marked "End" and then hide the thread ends in the tatting stitches.

There is one more unused picot. Attach the leaf and stem to this picot.

Vintage Leaf

This leaf can be tatted in many variations by changing the length of the pearl tatting in the middle and number of chain stitches around the outline of the leaf between the joins to the twisted cord picots.

Paper Clip

This rose is perfect to sew onto a hanky. And wouldn't it look nice on a blouse or dress?

The leaf is started as pearl tatting. Begin with two threads about two or three yards long. Put one thread through a paper clip, and with the other begin pearl tatting. One stitch on one side, then one on the other, tatting over the threads that are through the paper clip.

Do four stitches on each side, then make a twisted cord picot by twisting the thread in the same direction as the twist of the thread. Do another stitch on the same side, and then one on the other side, and then a twisted cord picot on that side.

Do four more stitches and then another two twisted cord picots. Do five stitches and then another pair of twisted cord picots. Finish with about three more stitches on each side.

Leaf Outline

The shuttle thread is one of the threads that was used to make the stitches of the pearl tatting, and one of the threads from the middle of the pearl tatting is used as the ball thread.

Chain enough stitches to go past the first twisted cord picot, as shown, and then join to it.

Continue tatting chain stitches as shown, joining to the twisted cord picots.

At the point of the leaf join to the loop of thread that was around the paper clip, leave a picot, and then join to the same loop again. (Remove the paper clip first, of course!)

Continue tatting the other side of the leaf outline as shown.

When you get back to the bottom of the leaf add in the other two threads to the core and tat Balanced Double Stitches over all three core threads to the desired length for the leaf stem. Join to the rose and then continue tatting the stem of the rose.

No two of these leaves will be exactly the same. The shape will depend upon the length of the twisted cord picots, and the number of stitches between them, and the stitches between them in the outline.

Skill Level: Beginner

Daisy

Use a yellow shuttle thread and white ball thread.

Ring (2 - 2 - 2 - 2 - 2 - 2 - 2 - 2 - 2 - 2 - 2 - 2 - 2)
12 picots separated by 2 DS

Tie the yellow ends to form the 13th picot. Turn

Chain (12-12) This forms the petal.

Join to the same picot of the center ring, and then join to the next picot of the center ring.

Repeat petals around until each picot of the center ring has a petal.

Note these petals should be long and narrow with a point at the picot in the center. Tie like color thread ends together.

Flower Center

Ring 1 (1 - 1 - 1 - 1 - 1 - 1 - 1 - 1 - 1 - 1 - 1 - 1) eleven large picots.

Ring 2 (1 - 1 - 1 - 1 - 1 - 1) five medium picots.

Assemble the flower as shown above by inserting the thread ends of the center through the middle of the petals.

Six Petal Flower

Skill Level: Intermediate

This six petal flower has a center round of rings and chains and an outer round of rings, chains, and split rings. It can be tatted in one, two or three colors (as shown in this sample). If tatted in just one color, you can use a split ring to climb out of the first round.

Center Round

First Ring (2 - 3 - 4 -- 4 - 3 - 2) Turn

Chain 4 Turn

Ring (2 + 3 + 4 -- 4 - 3 - 2) Turn

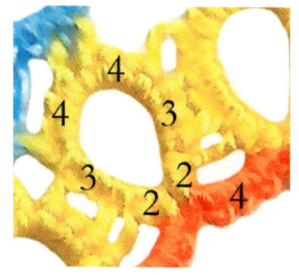

Repeat Chain and Ring around, joining the 12th ring to the first.

Tie like color thread ends together.
Hide the ends. Cut close to the work.

Round Two

Begin with the large ring at the middle of the petal as shown.

Large Ring A (4 - 5 - 2 - 2 - 5 - 4) Turn

Chain 4 Turn

Small Ring B (4 + 4 - 4 - 4) Turn

Chain 4 Turn

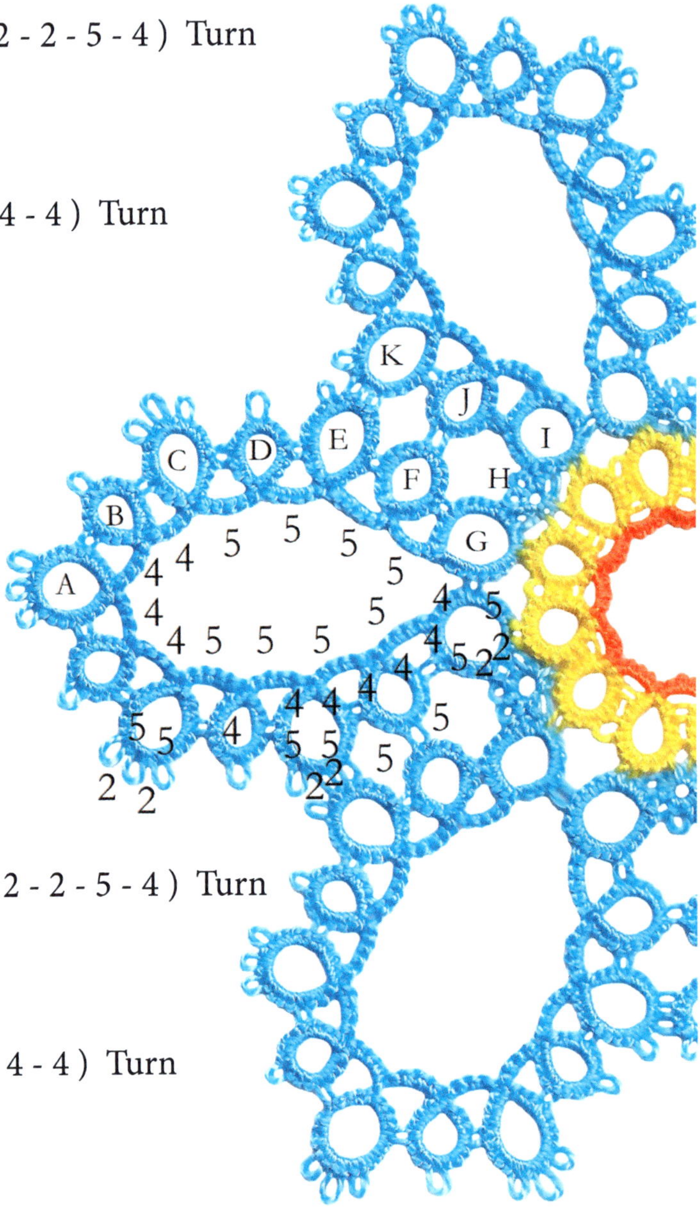

Large Ring C (4 + 5 - 2 - 2 - 5 - 4) Turn

Chain 5 Turn

Small Ring D (4 + 4 - 4 - 4) Turn

Chain 5 Turn

Large Joining Ring E (4 + 5 - 2 - 2 - 5 - 4) Turn

Chain 5 Turn

14

Small Joining Ring F (4 + 5 - 5 - 4) Turn

Chain 5

Sh #2 Large Split Ring G (4 - 5 + 2 - 2 / 4 + 5)

Small Flower Split Ring H (1 + 1 + 1 - 1 / 1 - 1 - 1)

Large Split Ring I (2 + 2 + 5 - 4 / 5 - 4) Turn

Chain 5 Turn

Small Joining Ring J (4 + 5 + 5 - 4) Turn

Chain 5 Turn

Large Joining Ring K (4 + 5 + 2 + 2 - 5 - 4) Turn

Chain 5 Turn,

Small Ring (4 + 4 - 4 - 4) Turn,

Chain 5 Turn

Large Ring (4 + 5 - 2 - 2 - 5 - 4) Turn

Chain 4

Small Ring (4 + 4 - 4 - 4) Turn

Chain 4.

Repeat from beginning of round two around, joining as shown.

THC

X ← Center

The photo above shows the detail of the split rings used to climb out of the center to the outside round. Begin this center with a picot by tying an overhand knot in the thread between the two shuttles. Tat the first DS a picot's distance from the knot.

Chain - 4 Turn [This chain is indicated with an " x " on the photo.]

Ring (2 - 3 - 4 - 4 - 3 - 2) Turn

Chain 4 Turn

Ring (2 + 3 + 4 - 4 - 3 - 2) Turn

Repeat rings and chains around joining the 12th (split) ring to the previous ring and to the first ring. To do this tat the last chain 4, join to the beginning picot, and then tat the 12th Split Ring (2 + 2 + 4 / 2 + 3 + 4)

Leave a thread space the size of a picot as shown in the photo above.

First Split ring of the outside round (5 - 4 / 2 - 2 - 5 - 4) Turn

Chain 5 Turn

Detail of the split Rings where the petals join to the center.

Center

This photo shows the detail of the three split rings where the petals join to the center. Shuttle two is used to tat the part of each of these split rings that actually joins to the center. Shuttle one is used to tat the second part of each ring.

Each petal has six of the smaller rings including two of the joining rings that have 4 5 5 4 stitch counts instead of 4 4 4 4. Each petal also has seven of the larger rings including the two split rings that join to the center.

The small flower split rings are between the petals. There is only one DS between the picots and joins in the small flower rings.

Circle Flower

Skill Level: Beginner

Wind two shuttles, CTM Continuous Thread Method Do NOT cut the thread between the two shuttles.

Each motif does not require two full shuttles to tat. Try a sample to determine how much you will need for the thread you are using.

Center

Ring 5 large picots sep by 2 DS

Leave a space the size of a large picot before tatting the split ring to begin the second row.

Second Round

Split Ring (2 - 2 - 2 / 2 - 2 - 2) turn

*

Chain (2 - 2 - 2 - 2) turn

Ring (2 - 2 + 2 - 2 - 2 - 2) turn

Chain (2 - 2 - 2 - 2) turn

Ring (2 + 2 - 2 + 2 - 2 - 2) turn
*

Repeat between ** around, as shown in the photo.

Circle Flower Table Mat

Skill Level:
Beginner

This lacy table mat can be made to about any size you wish just by adding more motifs in each row, and adding more rows as desired.

With all those picots around the outside there are lots of options for joining. The simplest joins will be to the center picots in the groups of three picots around the outside.

You may tat an edging around the outside of the piece if you wish, Perhaps something that has scallops. An edging around the outside will also help to make the piece more stable and easier to wash and block.

Tatted Table Cloth

Skill Level: Intermediate

Smaller motifs may be combined and repeated to make larger projects in tatting with relative ease. There are a few things to consider before beginning a large project.

1. Tat a small sample as a practice piece, and to calculate the size desired and the amount of thread required,
2. Choose a VERY good quality of thread that works up nicely and has the feel and texture desired. Thread that is great for a doily may not be the "right" thread for making an item like a scarf that will be next to your skin. I hate wearing scratchy feeling things.
3. Purchase the quantity of thread plus a couple of extra balls of the thread, just in case, for the project at one time. Dye lots can vary some and putting hours and hours of work into something that will be just a little off color in the final corner is very frustrating.

To make a hexagon tablecloth 96" across:

If one motif is six inches across, you will need 16 motifs across.
96 / 6 = 16

The area of a circle is 3.14 (PI) times the radius squared.
The Diameter is 16, so the radius is half of 16 or 8.
8 x 8 = 64   64 x 3.14 = 200.96

So you will need about 201 motifs to complete the piece. Add more if you plan to tat an edging around the outside. If one ball of thread will make about six motifs, then it will take about 34 balls of thread to complete the piece. 201 / 6 = 33.5

This is a good guess... But, ALWAYS buy extra to allow for errors, and unexpected issues with the thread.

Some motifs joined in rows are not the same measurement in both directions because of the way they are joined together.

This doily is three motifs across in every direction, but there are two motifs in one row and three in the next, then two again.

This six point motif will not easily make a "round" tablecloth. It will, however, make a hexagon tablecloth appropriate for a round table. The drawing below shows a hexagon that has 127 flower motifs.
It measures 78" across when tatted with a six" motif.

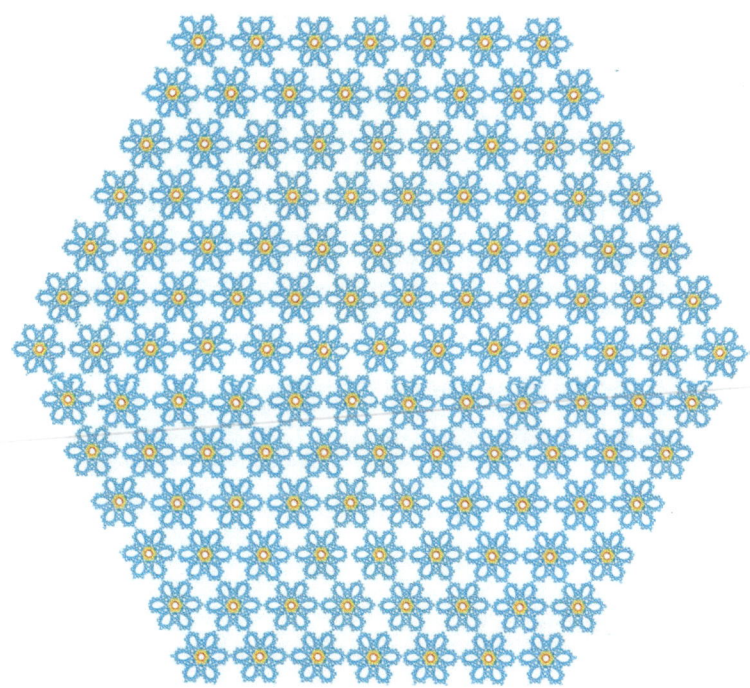

To tat a truly round tablecloth begin with a round motif and add rows of tatted edgings, keeping it a circle. Don't be afraid to try new things. Some edgings are more easily added to a tablecloth because they are more flexible, and will bend as much as necessary for the circle.

   I think any tatted tablecloth would look beautiful on a round table!

Designing A Round Tablecloth

The circle flower on page 18 will make a beautiful beginning for a round table cloth. Next, add a row of the rings and chains with the rings only joined to the center picots of the previous row, not joined to the other rings. You will need to alter the stitch counts for the chains to make it "fit" the spaces between the rings.

You can either add stitches at the beginning and end of each chain section or add more stitches and picots to each chain section.

One row of the shell edging on page 48 is very flexible and would make a nice row around the circle at any place you choose to use it.

Worst case in trying something is this: Try it, and if you don't like the look after just a bit of tatting, cut it off and try something else. There is so much satisfaction when you finally find the perfect fit!!!

You can be a tatting designer! Yes you can.

Tatted Wine Glass Marker

Begin with one shuttle and ball CTM. Do not cut the thread from the ball.

You will need a little more than a circle of memory wire which can be purchased at a craft store, and about 50 small pearl beads, or beads of your choice, and one slightly larger bead.

Skill Level: Beginner

Fasten the thread to the memory wire by putting a lrage bead on the tatting thread and use jewelry glue to fasten it on one ned of the memory wire.

Chain 4 - 1 - 1 - 4

Slide three small pearl beads onto the wire and around to the where the last DS is on the wire.

Do a shuttle join to the wire, and then repeat the tatting around the memory wire.

The sample above is shown just needing the last three small beads. It does not have the first bead. Glue a larger bead to cover each end.

Slide the larger bead onto the threads, and then onto the memory wire. Fasten it to the wire with a bit of jewelery glue and when dry cut the thread. Make these in a variety of colors and use to identify your wine glass when you have your next get together with friends.

You may substitute any edging pattern for this tatting to make a variety of designs for your enjoyment.

Skill Level:
Intermediate

Three Flowers Heart

This simple little heart is tatted in two rounds. The first is the three flowers in the center, and the second is the heart outline.

This sample is tatted in two colors, each with one shuttle and ball CTM. The thread I used is Lizbeth size 20 and the finished sample is about 2.25 inches across.

Begin a tatted chain with a picot. Tie a knot in the thread between the ball and shuttle, then tat the first DS a picot's distance from the knot. The diagram on the next page shows an X at the center where you start. Follow the arrows and letters for the progression of the tatting.

A   Chain – 6 – 2 Turn

B   Ring (2 – 2 – 2 – 2 – 2 – 2 – 2 – 2 – 2 – 2 – 2 – 2) Turn
There are eleven picots in this ring.

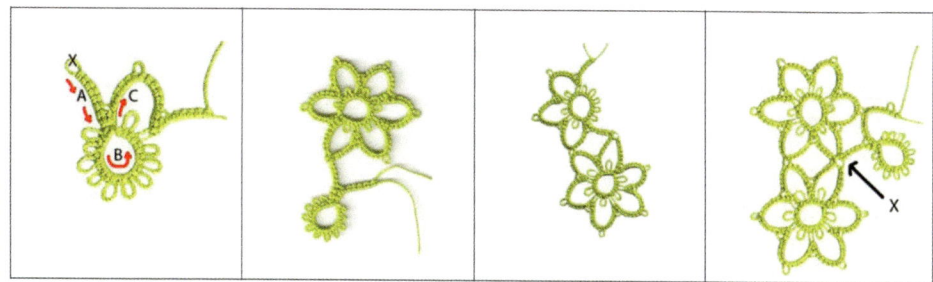

C Chain 2 + 6 – 6 – 2 + The first join is to the last picot of the previous chain, and the second join is to a picot of the ring, skip one picot, join to the next.

D Repeat the chains and joins around to complete the first flower.

E The final chain of the first flower. Join into the beginning picot at X.

F Begin the second flower: Chain 6 – 2 Turn

G Ring (2 – 2 – 2 – 2 – 2 – 2 – 2 – 2 – 2 – 2 – 2 – 2) Turn
There are eleven picots.

H Chain 2 + 6 + 6 – 2 + The first join is to the last picot of the previous chain, and the second join is to the picot of the first flower. The third join is to the picot of the ring, skipping one as before.

I Repeat the chains and joins around to complete the second flower. Join into the beginning picot at X.

J Begin the third flower: Chain 6 – 2 Turn, Ring, Continue as before.

25

K, L, M, N… The third flower is a repeat of the second flower except that it joins to the second flower, also to the first flower. Finally, Cut the thread ends leaving about 10" and then tie the ends in the beginning picot at X.

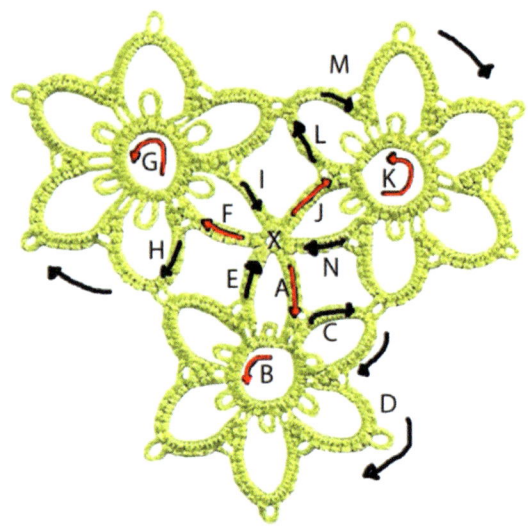

Outline Round

Join into the picot where any two of the center flowers join together.

Chain 2 – 3 – 3 – 3 – 3 +
This join is to the next petal of the same flower. Leave a picot space and do not tat the second half of the joining DS. Instead tat a full DS next which will leave a nice symmetrical picot at the join.

Chain 3 – 3 – 3 – 3 +
Repeat the previous chain and join to the next petal as before. The next chain has seven picots between the joins.

Chain 3 – 3 – 3 – 3 – 3 – 3 – 3 – 3 +

Chain 3 – 3 – 3 – 3 – 1 +

At the bottom point of the heart leave a slightly larger picot.
Continue… Chain 1 – 3 – 3 – 3 – 3 +

The second side of the heart is a mirror image of the first. Ending the heart back at the top. Join to the first picot of this row, and then chain 2 DS, cut the thread ends leaving about 10" of thread to tie back into the same picot of the flowers where the outline row began.

Tiny Beaded Heart

Skill Level: Beginner

This heart is just rings with three beads that make it curve into a heart.

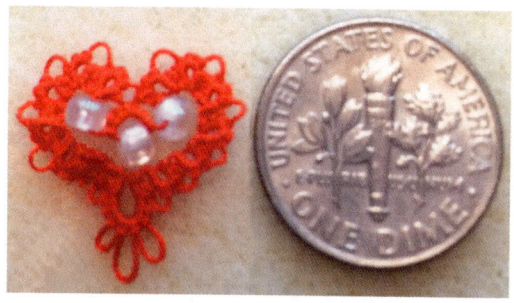

Slide three beads onto the thread of a shuttle wound with any size & color thread. The beads should be just large enough to string on the thread. The picots between rings are all very small ones. The three picots in the center of the bottom ring are larger.

Ring1 (2 - 2 - 2)

Ring2 (2 + 3 - 2) Join to last picot of previous ring.

Repeat Ring2 three more times.

Slide a bead next to the ring just made.
Slide a bead onto the thread used to make this next ring: Ring (3 + 3)
Slide a bead next to the ring just made.

Ring (2 + 3 - 2) This one is the same as ring2 & it joins to the same picot as the last ring did. There are three rings joined together here.

Repeat Ring2 three more times.

Ring (2 + 2 - 2)
Repeat this ring once.

Ring (2 + 3 - 1 - 1 - 3 - 2) This is the point at the bottom of the heart.

Ring (2 + 2 + 2) This is the last ring. It is joined to the previous ring and the first ring.
THC

Skill Level: Beginner

Clovers Heart

This is a pretty easy little heart to tat. Each side of the heart is tatted individually, and the ring at the bottom is only tatted with the first side.

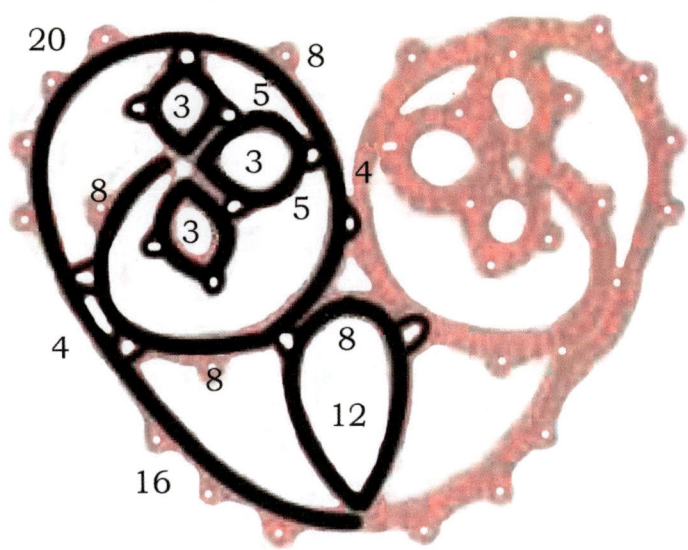

Begin with any size and color of thread wound on a shuttle and ball CTM

*

Clover

Ring1 (3 - 3 - 3 - 3)
Ring2 (3 + 5 - 5 - 3)
Ring3 (3 + 3 - 3 - 3) turn

Chain (8 - 4 - 8 - 8 - 4 + 8 + 20 + 4 + 16) turn
*

Ring (12 + 8 - 12)

Leave the thread ends long enough to hide, or longer to make twisted cord for a bookmark.

Tat the other side of the heart, between the ** in the instructions above, joining to the first half were shown on the photo diagram.

THC

Heart Sachet

Skill Level:
Beginner

This heart is just rings, chains, and joins with the option to cut and tie after the first round or climb out to the second round with one split ring to make it an advanced beginner level project.

Beginners should find this easy to do as there is just one split ring and it makes it SO much easier to tat one split ring than to hide the extra two thread ends. OK, I confess, I can be lazy at times.

The stitch counts for this heart are the same as the hearts for the Pearl Butterfly, but without any beads.

Tat two hearts, and then cut out two smaller hearts from a fine net or other material such as used dryer sheets or a sheer fabric of your choice.

Sew them together leaving a small opening along one of the sides to fill with lavender buds. Stitch the opening. Place the lavender filled pouch between the two tatted hearts and sew through the rings of both hearts with a fine ribbon.

Tie the ribbon at the top and use it to hang the sachet in your closet or tie the ribbons in a bow and place it in a drawer.

You may purchase lavender from my friends Amy & Kim here: http://onederings.com

Some of their lavender plants came from the lavender along the walk at our home in Ohio. We had a LOT of lavender!!!

You may wish to make it with more of a frilly look by making a picot between each of the DS in the chains around the outline.

You may even make five picots between the rings with one DS between picots. For a nicle scalloped edge, vary the length of the picots; small, medium, large, medium, small.

Skill Level:
   Intermediate

Pearl Butterfly

The butterfly requires two hearts that are joined to the body as they are tatted. The larger pearl beads are sewn on when you sew the butterfly onto fabric. If you have missed any of the smaller beads while tatting the hearts, they may be added at this time as well.

> I sewed this butterfly onto the pocket of my blue jean jacket, but wouldn't it look stunning on a ring bearer pillow for a wedding with ribbons at the bottom wings to tie on the rings?

There is one split ring to climb out of the first row of the heart, however, it can be tatted with one shuttle and the ball of thread for the second shuttle for that one split ring. Beginners can eliminate the split ring, and cut the thread ends after the first round. Just leave enough thread to tie the ends to the second round when the piece is finished.

You may tat the hearts first and then join them to the body as it is tatted, or tat the body first, and join to the hearts as they are tatted.

Body

Put five small pearl beads on your thread and then wind two shuttles CTM with a yard or two each.

Begin at the tip of the abdomen by tatting a ring with beads on it. Slide four small pearl beads onto the thread around your hand. One bead remains on the shuttle 1 thread.

S1 Ring (1 - 5 [put three beads on the picot, and slide the one bead from the shuttle thread up on the core thread before making the next DS.] 5 - 1) Close the ring with the fifth bead still on the core thread.

Split Ring (1 + 6 - 1 / 1 + 6 - 1)

Split Ring (1 + 3 - 3 - 1 / 1 + 3 - 3 - 1)

Repeat the first split ring two more times.

Split Ring Thorax (1 + 4 - 4 - 1 / 1 + 4 - 4 - 1)

Head & Antennae

Split Ring (1 + 4 / 1 + 4)

Add another piece of thread and tat the chains for the antennae: Chain 15 for each side, or to desired length.

Tie double overhand knots in each antennae thread ends. Cut. There are no ends to hide in this butterfly body!

For each heart, load about 70 small pearl beads onto the thread, and then wind one shuttle and ball CTM.

Slide seven of the beads onto the shuttle thread, and leave the rest of them on the ball thread. You will need about 25 additional small beads to add as you are joining.

Round One

Begin the heart with a picot by tying an overhand knot in the thread between the ball and shuttle. Make the first DS a picot's distance from the knot.

Tie an overhand knot in the two threads after the chain 4 to hold the DS in place.

Chain A – 4 turn

Ring (6 – 6 B 5 – 5) turn

Chain 6 – 6 turn

Ring (4 + 4 – 4 – 4) turn

Chain 8 – 4 – 6 turn

Ring (4 + 4 – 4) turn

Chain 6 – 4 – 8 turn

Ring (4 + 4 + 4 – 4) turn

Chain 6 – 6 turn

Ring (5 + 5 + 6 – 6) turn

Chain 4

34

Round Two

Leave a small space and tat the following split ring.
Split RingB (3 – 3 / 3 – 3) turn

Chain 2 B 2 B 2 B 2 turn

Ring (3 B+ 3 B+ 3 – 3) turn

Slide one bead onto the ring thread.
Ring (3 B+ 3 B 3 – 3) turn

Chain 2 B 2 B 2 B 2 turn

Continue tatting the rings and chains around. From Split Ring B there are four repeats of the small rings, with Chains between them to the bottom point of the heart.

The point at the bottom of the heart.

Ring (3 B+ 2 B 2 – 2 – 3) turn

Chain 2 B 2 B 2 B 2 – 2 B 2 B 2 B 2 turn

Notice that there is a PICOT at the very point of the heart. This is where the butterfly body joins to the heart for each wing. The body also joins to a picot along the side of each heart, but this join can be to a picot that has a bead on it.

Ring (3 B+ 2 B+ 2 B 2 B+ 3) turn

Follow the diagram around the heart. The second side is the mirror image of the first side, but tatted in reverse order from the point at the bottom back to the beginning at the top.

Heart Photo Frame

Skill Level: Advanced Beginner

Wind two tatting shuttles with thread, CTM. The sample is size 20 thread and about 3" tall. Begin with the clover at the top point of the heart.

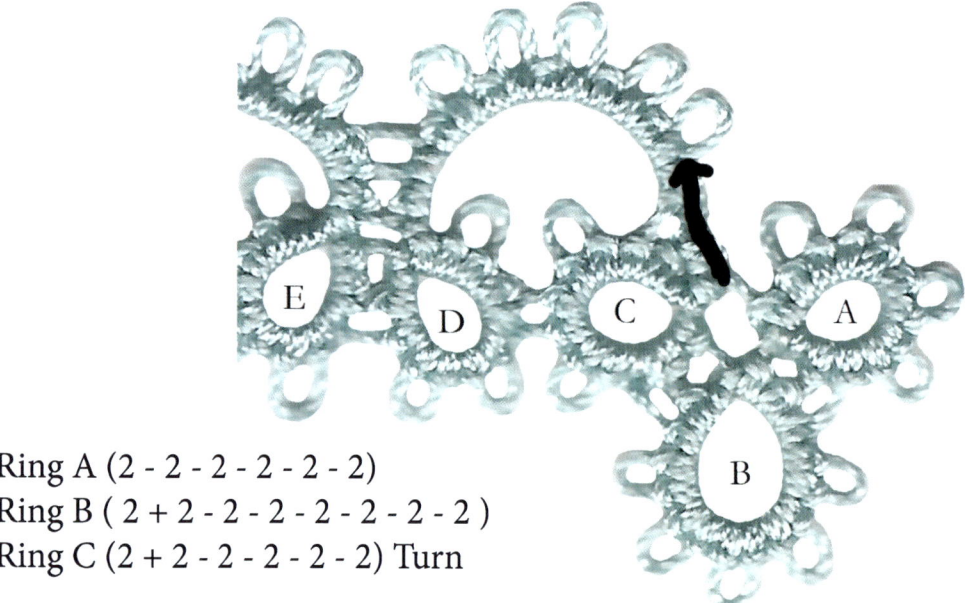

Ring A (2 - 2 - 2 - 2 - 2 - 2)
Ring B (2 + 2 - 2 - 2 - 2 - 2 - 2 - 2)
Ring C (2 + 2 - 2 - 2 - 2 - 2) Turn

Chain (2 + 2 - 2 - 2 - 2 - 2 - 2 - 2) Turn
The join is to the last picot of Ring C. 7 picots in this chain.
We are counting joins with the picots in all of these chains.

Ring D (2 - 2 - 2 + 2 - 2 - 2)
Ring E (2 + 2 - 2 - 2 - 2 - 2) Turn

Chain (2 + 2 - 2 - 2 - 2 - 2 - 2 - 2 - 2) Turn
The Join is to the last picot of the previous chain. 8 picots in this chain

Ring (2 - 2 + 2 + 2 - 2 - 2)
Ring (2 + 2 - 2 - 2 - 2 - 2) Turn

Chain (2 + 2 - 2 - 2 - 2 - 2 - 2 - 2 - 2 - 2) Turn
The join is to the last picot of the previous chain. 9 picots in this chain

Ring (2 - 2 + 2 + 2 - 2 - 2)
Ring (2 + 2 - 2 - 2 - 2 - 2) Turn

Chain (2 + 2 - 2 - 2 - 2 - 2 - 2 - 2 - 2 - 2) Turn
The join is to the last picot of the previous chain. 9 picots in this chain

Ring (2 - 2 + 2 + 2 - 2 - 2)
Ring (2 + 2 - 2 - 2 - 2 - 2) Turn

Chain (2 + 2 - 2 - 2 - 2 - 2 - 2 - 2 - 2) Turn
The join is to the last picot of the previous chain. 8 picots in this chain

Ring (2 - 2 + 2 + 2 - 2 - 2)
Ring (2 + 2 - 2 - 2 - 2 - 2) Turn

Chain (2 + 2 - 2 - 2 - 2 - 2 - 2 - 2 - 2) Turn
The join is to the last picot of the previous chain. 8 picots in this chain

Ring (2 - 2 + 2 + 2 - 2 - 2)
Ring (2 + 2 - 2 - 2 - 2 - 2) Turn

Chain (2 + 2 - 2 - 2 - 2 - 2 - 2 - 2) Turn
The join is to the last picot of the previous chain. 7 picots in this chain

Ring (2 - 2 + 2 + 2 - 2 - 2)
Ring (2 + 2 - 2 - 2 - 2 - 2) Turn

Chain (2 + 2 - 2 - 2 - 2 - 2 - 2 - 2) Turn
The join is to the last picot of the previous chain. 7 picots in this chain

Point at the bottom of the heart.

Ring (2 - 2 + 2 + 2 - 2 - 2)
Shuttle2 Ring (2 + 2 - 2 - 2 - 2 - 2 - 2 - 2)
Ring (2 + 2 - 2 - 2 - 2 - 2) Turn

Shuttle 1 rings

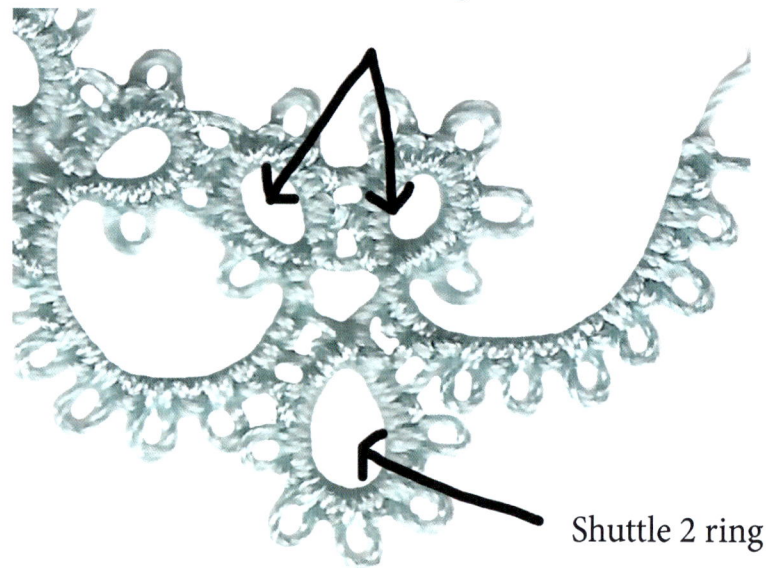

Shuttle 2 ring

The rest of the heart is the mirror image of what is already tatted,

Chain (2 + 2 - 2 - 2 - 2 - 2 - 2 - 2) Turn
The join is to the last picot of the Shuttle 2 ring.   7 picots in this chain

Ring (2 - 2 + 2 + 2 - 2 - 2)
Ring (2 + 2 - 2 - 2 - 2 - 2) Turn

Chain (2 + 2 - 2 - 2 - 2 - 2 - 2 - 2) Turn
The join is to the last picot of the previous chain.   7 picots in this chain

Ring (2 - 2 + 2 + 2 - 2 - 2)
Ring (2 + 2 - 2 - 2 - 2 - 2) Turn

Chain (2 + 2 - 2 - 2 - 2 - 2 - 2 - 2) Turn
The join is to the last picot of the previous chain.   8 picots in this chain

Ring (2 - 2 + 2 + 2 - 2 - 2)
Ring (2 + 2 - 2 - 2 - 2 - 2)   Turn

Chain (2 + 2 - 2 - 2 - 2 - 2 - 2 - 2) Turn
The join is to the last picot of the previous chain.   8 picots in this chain

Ring (2 - 2 + 2 + 2 - 2 - 2)
Ring (2 + 2 - 2 - 2 - 2 - 2)   Turn

Chain (2 + 2 - 2 - 2 - 2 - 2 - 2 - 2) Turn
The join is to the last picot of the previous chain.   9 picots in this chain

Ring (2 - 2 + 2 + 2 - 2 - 2)
Ring (2 + 2 - 2 - 2 - 2 - 2)   Turn

Chain (2 + 2 - 2 - 2 - 2 - 2 - 2 - 2 - 2) Turn
The join is to the last picot of the previous chain.   9 picots in this chain

Ring (2 - 2 + 2 + 2 - 2 - 2)
Ring (2 + 2 - 2 - 2 - 2 - 2)   Turn

Chain (2 + 2 - 2 - 2 - 2 - 2 - 2 - 2) Turn
The join is to the last picot of the previous chain.   8 picots in this chain

Ring (2 - 2 + 2 + 2 - 2 - 2)
Ring (2 + 2 - 2 - 2 + 2 - 2)   Turn
The first join is to the previous ring.
The second join is to the third picot of Ring A

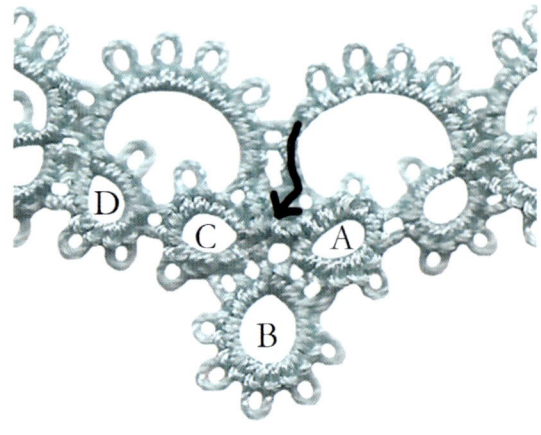

Chain (2 + 2 - 2 - 2 - 2 - 2 + 2 + 2)
7 picots (or joins) in this chain

This last chain section joins to the previous chain,
to the first chain, and then to the first picot of ring A.
Tie the ends at the beginning clover
where the first chain begins.. THC

Square Photo Frame

Similar to the heart, this square may be tatted following the same idea.

The rings join where shown in the photo, and the chains have seven picots along the sides and eleven at the corners. The chains are not joined together in this sample, but a variation would be to join the chains together as in the heart Photo frame.

Make this any size desired by making the sides longer.

Skill Level: Beginner

This is an old edging pattern that has been around for a long time.
It is very flexible and will easily make many different shapes
in addition to the heart and square.

In tiny thread it is a delicate edging for baby things or a nightie. It would look beautiful on a hanky as well as making a lovely insertion.

Skill Level:
Intermediate

Tatted Bed Spread

To make a bedspread you will need to decide the size of the bed. For instance a twin bed is 39" by 75" for a standard US mattress, and a bedspread with the overhang is about 65" x 88".

There are standard sizes for commercial bedding, and also a very nice size chart for making quilts online here:

http://www.generations-quilt-patterns.com/standard-quilt-sizes.html

If you are tatting a square motif that is 6" by 6" it is easy to figure out that 65 / 6 = 10.83 and 88 / 6 = 14.66 so you will need ten or eleven motifs by 14 or 15 motifs to make the piece. Ten x 15 is 150 motifs. If a ball of thread will make six motifs you will need 25 balls of thread. But **ALWAYS** add a few and buy enough for the entire project plus extra. You can use the extra thread when you are finished to make matching pillowcase edgings, doilies, or whatever accessories desired for the room. There are several lovely edgings that would look great on a pillowcase in this book.

These calculations may vary depending upon the motif selected, and if you want to add an edging all around the bedspread. Tat a row across the shorter measurement to see how many repeats of the pattern you want to make, and then see how many times that measurement is needed for the longer side. Tatting often is very lacy and has a lot of white space, so it looks dainty and elegant.

When I was a teenager back in the 60s people would tell me that I should make tablecloths and bedspreads and sell them. "Someone would probably be willing to pay $25 for a bedspread!", they would say.

 So, if the thread cost $50 and it took me 200 hours I would only get half of the cost of the thread, and spend hundreds of hours to tat it. Wait, it's a labor of love!!! Right?

Here is a square motif that can be tatted to whatever size required. The sample here is four inches across each square in size 8 perle cotton.

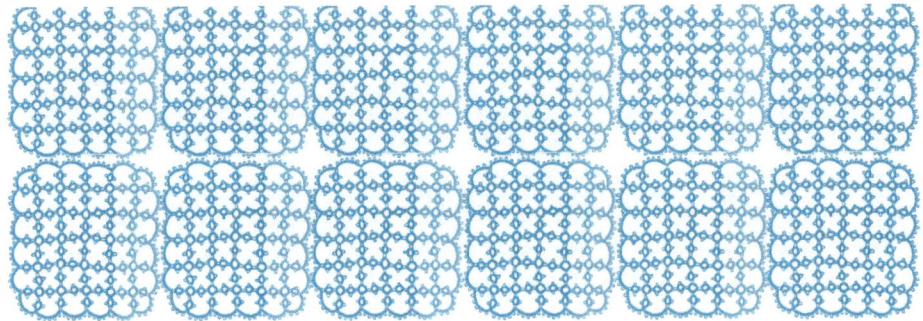

Each square is tatted separately and joined together as the outside round is tatted. The squares are just rings, split rings, and joins, with the outside round just chains. Begin with two shuttles wound CTM in any size and color thread.

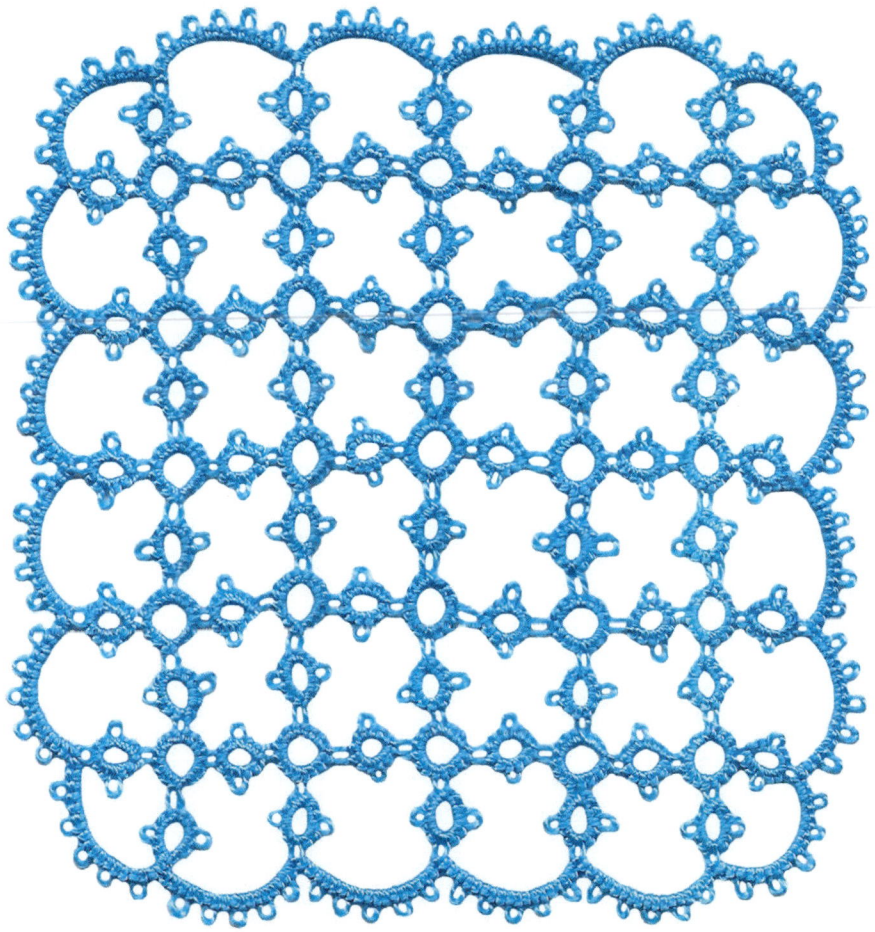

43

Endles Tatted Squares

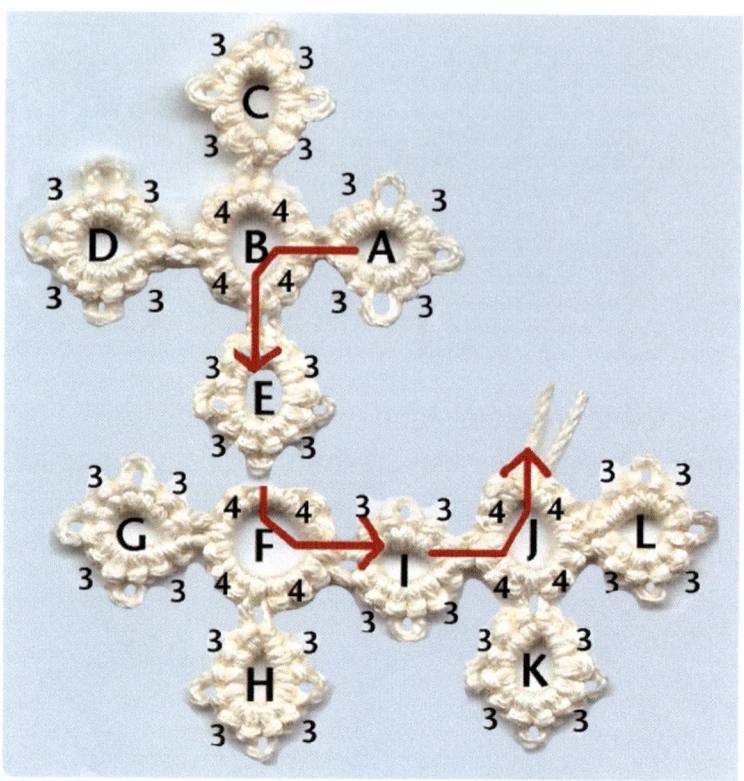

Ring A (3 – 3 – 3 – 3)

Split Ring B (4 / 4 (thrown off ring C) 4 (thrown off ring D) 4)

Split Ring E (3 – 3 / 3 – 3)

Split Ring F (4 / 4 (thrown off ring G) 4 (thrown off ring H) 4)

Split Ring I (3 – 3 / 3 – 3)

Split Ring J (4 / 4 (thrown off ring K) 4 (thrown off ring L) 4)

Split Ring M (3 – 3 / 3 – 3)

Split Ring N (4 – 4 / 4 (thrown off ring O) 4)

This pattern incorporates rings, split rings, and thrown off rings to create an endless square. Tat with two shuttles CTM. Use any size and any color of thread desired.

The letters and arrows indicate the progression of the tatting. The numbers show the stitch counts. Notice that there are split rings with all stitch counts of 4, and rings, thrown off rings, and split rings with all stitch counts of 3.

SR N is different than the previous split rings with the 4 stitches because it joins in the first half of the ring to the first Ring A.

Continue tatting following the pattern diagrams to the desired size. Always go in the spiral around as shown.

When the piece is as large as desired you may tat a row around the outside to give the edge a more solid look. Tat chains with five picots sep by 3 DS, between the rings around as shown on page 43.

Skill Level: Beginner

Antique Edging & Insertion

This simple little edging is similar to one that my mother used to tat to sew on my clothes. She made yards and yards of it!

One shuttle and ball CTM

Ring (3 – 3 – 3 – 3) Turn

***

Chain 9 – 6 – 3 Turn

Ring (3 – 3 + 3 – 3) Turn

Chain 3 Turn

Ring (3 + 5 – 1 – 1 – 5 – 3) Turn

Chain 3 Turn

Ring (3 + 3 – 3 – 3) Turn

Chain 3 + 6 – 9 Turn

Ring (3 + 3 – 3 – 3) Turn

Repeat from *** to desired length

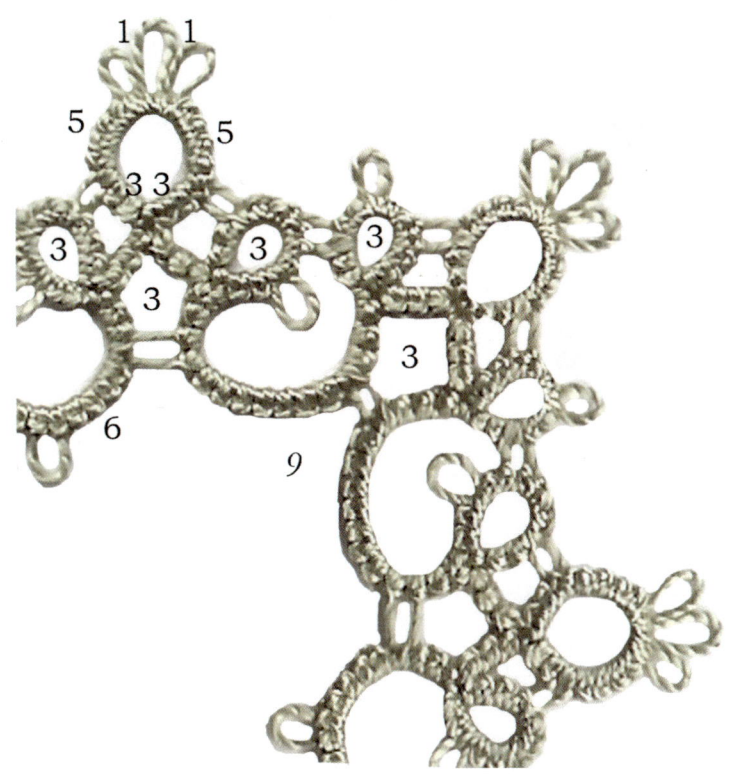

Edging Corner

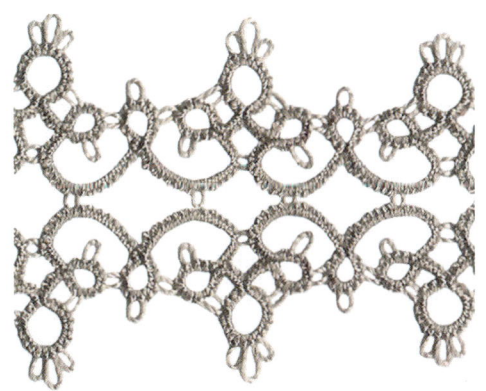

Insertion Lace

Skill Level: Intermediate

Shell Edging

Start with Shuttle 1
Ring A (8 – 4 – 4 – 8)

Shuttle 2
Split Ring B (4 – 4 /2 RC 2 RD 2 RE 2)

Rings C, D, & E are thrown off rings tatted with shuttle 1.

Turn the work over to tat the 2 DS between Rings:

RC, RD, & RE (8 + 4 – 4 – 8) Turn

Shuttle 1
Split Ring F R (8 + 4 / 8 – 4)

The pattern repeats from Ring G on to the desired length.

Shuttle 1 Split Ring G SR (4 – 8 / 4 – 8)

Shuttle 2
Split Ring H SR (4 – 4 / 2 RI 2 RJ 2 RK 2)

The next Split ring is a repeat of Ring F, and continue on to the desired length, These may be tatted in stacked rows with the picot of Ring B joined to the previous row Ring D picot.

Shell Scarf or Table Runner

Each shell is three split rings and three normal rings. When the rows are "stacked" or repeated one on top of the other a larger project may continue endlessly.

These samples are tatted with three neutral colors of size 20 Lisbeth thread. Each shell is about 1 1/4" wide by 3/4" high.
Five rows make it a little more than three inches tall, and 40 shells across is about 50" wide.

Skill Level:
Beginner

Pantry Shelf Vintage Lace

This is another variation on a very old edging pattern. It is tatted in multiple rows. There are three rows shown in the photo above, but it can be anything from one row to a hundred or more rows.

The negative spaces in the photo are as beautiful as the lace that is tatted to make this pattern. Add beads if you wish, to make a beautiful bracelet or choker.

Begin with one shuttle and ball of thread CTM. Do not cut the thread from the ball.

Ring (1 - 1 - 1 - 1 - 1 - 1 - 1 - 1) Turn
Chain 12 - 6 + 6 Turn
Ring (1 - 1 - 1 - 1 - 1 - 1) Turn
Chain 6 Turn
Ring (1 - 1 - 1 - 1 - 1 - 1 - 1 - 1) Turn
Chain 6 + 12 + 6 Turn

Repeat to desired length.

The next row is joined as shown at the middle picot of the smaller rings, and has an extra picot in the chain sections where there are 12 DS in the chain in the first row, it is Chain 6 - 6 - 6 in the second row.

The photo above is a closer view of the lace. The bottom row of the sample is very much the same as the middle row except that the two rows join at the picots along the longer chains.

This lace was designed to be sewn onto a shelf liner and hang down in front of the shelves.

Oh SO shabby Chic !!!

Skill Level:
Intermediate

Ribbon & Flowers Lace

This tatted edging is designed so that a ribbon may be woven through under the flowers.

Two shuttles wound CTM (Continuous Thread Method) with any size and color of thread. This sample is size 20. The diagram photos are in two shades of aqua to show the split rings and shuttle2 rings that join to each other.

The tatting is done in two rounds with the flowers and connecting rings inside as the first round and the outside is the second round. However, the first round is tatted along one side then back along the other side with just half of each flower done first and the second half finishes the first round.

Begin the first round with the numbered split ring shown below. The final split ring of the first round is used to go from the first round to the second round.

The pattern repeats to desired length before doing the other half of the first round.

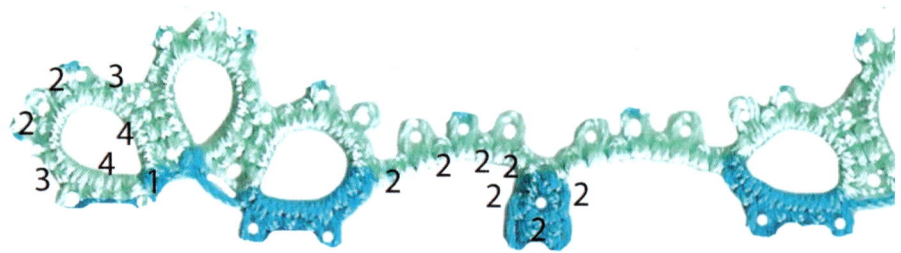

Ring (1 - 4 - 3 - 2 - 2 - 3 - 4)
*

Split Ring (4 + 3 - 2 - 2 - 3 - 4 / 1)
Split Ring (4 + 3 - 2 - 2 / 1 - 4 - 3) Turn

Chain 2 - 2 - 2 - 2 Turn
Ring (2 - 2 - 2) Turn
Chain 2 - 2 - 2 - 2 Turn

Split Ring (2 - 2 - 3 - 4 / 3 - 4 - 1)
*

Repeat between ** to desired length, and then work back across the length to complete the first round. Join where indicated on the photo.

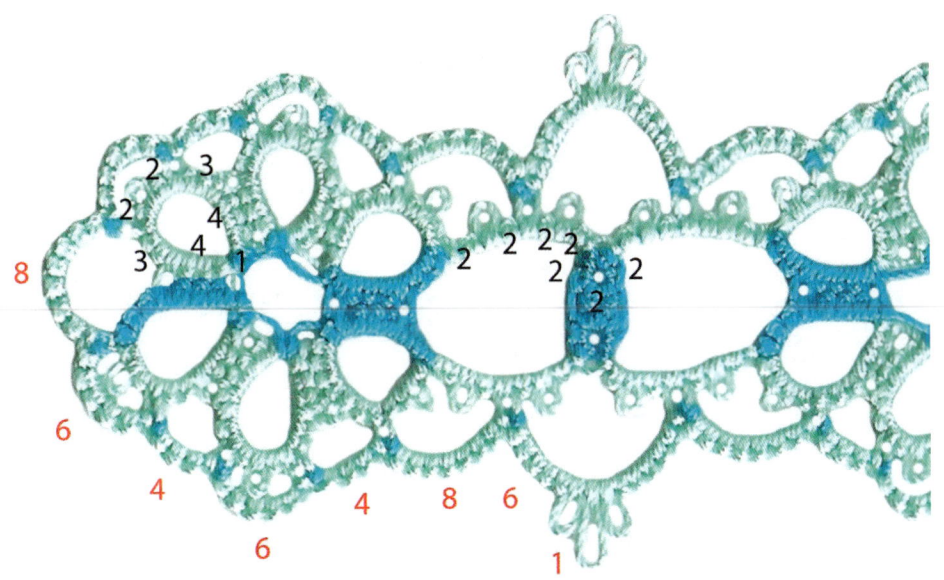

The black numbers are the stitch counts for the first round. The red numbers are the stitch counts for the outside (second round).

The thread colors show the use of shuttle1 and shuttle2 for the split rings. Notice the split ring at the bottom left. This is the split ring used to climb out of the first round.

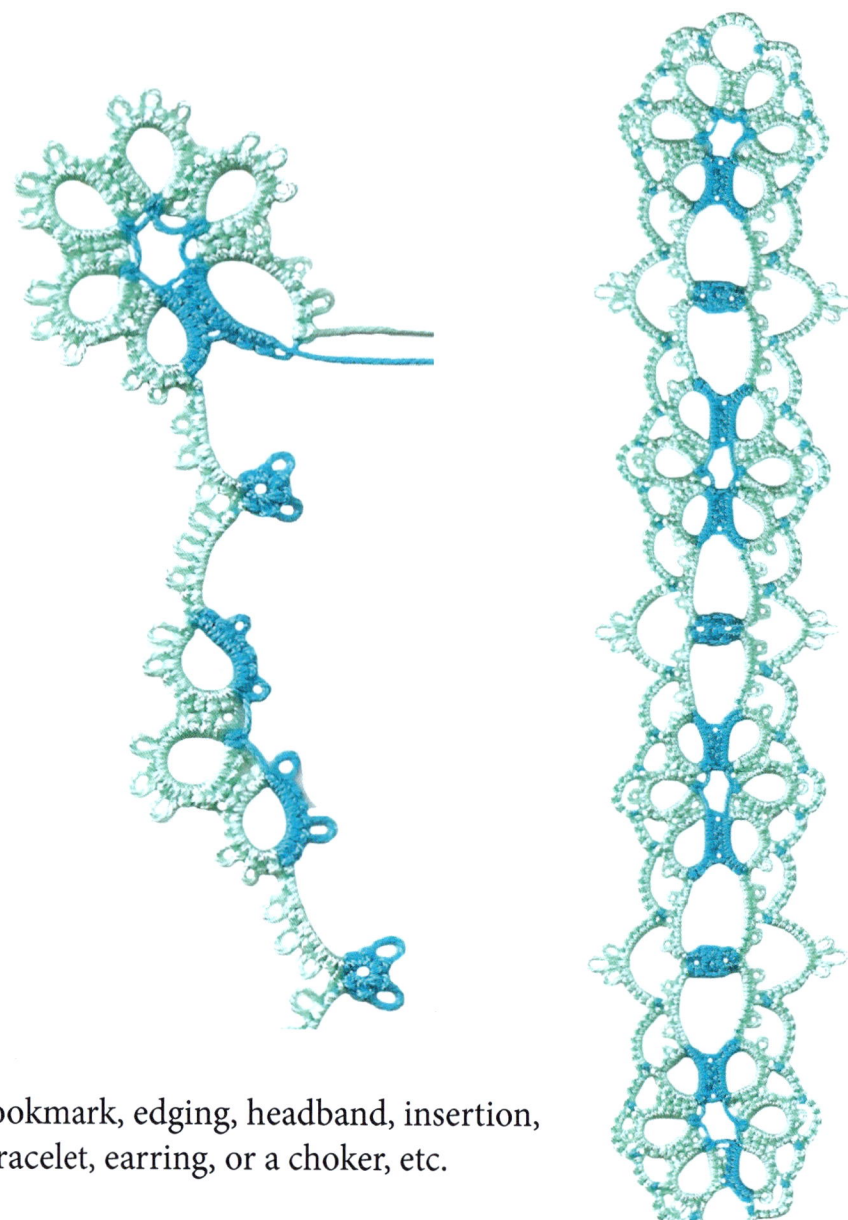

It is a bookmark, edging, headband, insertion, bracelet, earring, or a choker, etc.

The end flower continues like the small flower by tatting the other three rings. Next repeat the other side of the pattern, joining the small rings at both picots and the flowers at the two available joining picots of the first and third petal rings. The End Flower is almost completed here. The photo above left shows all the rings for the end flower tatted and the sixth ring being closed. Notice that the shuttle two (darker thread) is the core of the ring. I just find it easier to do the two joins to the first ring this way.

The next thing to do is the chain and then the shuttle 2 small ring. It joins to both picots of the mirror image ring already tatted. This makes the place for the ribbon to weave over so that it will weave under the flowers. Just continue on with tatting the mirror image of the first half of round one. When you get back to the beginning you will finish the second half of the flower at the beginning. Be sure to join to both picots of each of the split rings shown here with two joining picots. The middle ring in each group of three for the first half of round one does not join to the second half of the round. The middle ring of each group of three in the second half of round one only joins to the adjacent two rings as well.

You may add beads to the decorative picots and to the joining picots if you wish. You may even choose to add a beaded tatted flower to the center of the ribbon woven through if you wish.

The sample below has beads on the outside round, and a beaded flower sewn onto the embossed white ribbon.

You may cut and tie and then hide the ends, or make the final ring to complete the second half of the first round a split ring to climb out and begin the second (outside) round. Then continue around with:

Chain 6 + 4 + 6 + 4 + 8 + 6 - 1 - 1 - 6 + 8 + 4 + 6 +

This chain repeats all around the outside as shown in the diagram and photos.

Flower Edging Corner

Every edging needs to have a corner just in case you need to put it on a hanky or the yoke of a shirt. This is another variation on the simple flower design. It has eight rings instead of six. Tat it in line with the Flower Edging by simply substituting it for one of the six ring flowers in the edging. Wouldn't this look sexy sewn onto a V neck nightie?

Do you see a butterfly?

When using this flower to turn the corner in the edging it is easier to tat the inside two split rings of the corner before the outside six split rings.

Split Ring A (4 – 3 – 2 – 2 – 3 – 4 / 2)

Split Ring B (4 + 3 / 2 – 4 – 3 – 2 – 2)

Continue with the chains for the edging with ribbon weaving. When you are tatting the second half of round one tat the other six of the eight split rings.

The difference between these rings and the ones in the six ring flowers is that there are 2 stitches in each ring at the center of the flower instead of one.

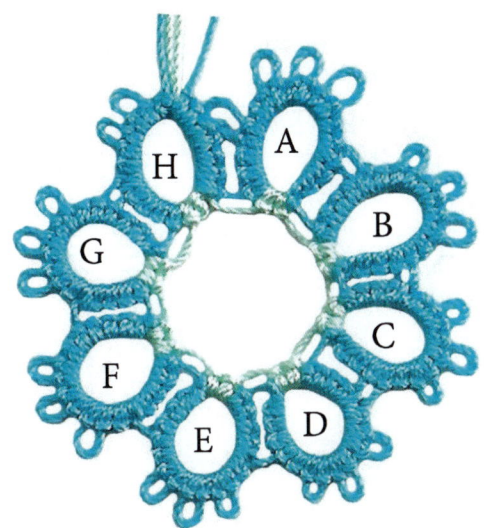

Eight split ring flower

Ring A (2 – 4 – 3 – 2 – 2 – 3 – 4)

Split Ring B (4 + 3 – 2 – 2 – 3 – 4 / 2)

Repeat Split Ring B five more times for Split Rings C, D, E, F, & G.

Split Ring H (4 + 3 – 2 – 2 / 2 (Shuttle 2) (4 + 3 Shuttle 1 tail))

The second part of this split ring is 2 reversed DS with the shuttle 2 thread, and then the 4 + 3 with the tail of the shuttle 1 thread, tatting over the shuttle 2 thread and tail.

You may adjust the end point where the threads all come out the top to be at the side joining picot or at the middle of the three picots at the top.

Skill Level:
Intermediate

Small Five Point Flower

Begin with two shuttles wound CTM.

Center Ring (2 B 2 R 2 B 2 R 2 B 2 R 2 B 2 R 2 B 2)

The rings thrown off by tatting with the second shuttle have three beads in the hand ring to start.

First Ring (2 - 6 BBB 6 - 2)

Ring 2,3,4 (2 + 6 BBB 6 - 2)

Final Split Ring (2 + 4 BBB 6 / 2 +)

Tie the thread ends in the picot of the first ring. Add a bead to the center of the flower when sewing it onto fabric or a tatted choker.

Printed in Great Britain
by Amazon.co.uk, Ltd.,
Marston Gate.